Contents

About the Author

An experienced digital marketing specialist and Member of the Chartered Institute of Marketing, Heather Robinson has over a decade of experience developing marketing strategies for businesses large and small.

Passionate about helping small businesses achieve their business goals and making digital marketing accessible to everyone, Heather is well placed to offer superior advice and expertise alongside hands-on, interactive training for business owners to really get to grips with social media platforms, the fundamentals of search engine optimisation and promoting their business online.

Heather is a regular speaker at conferences and events across the country including SES Conference and Biddable World in London, providing insights to her peers on a variety of digital marketing topics from social media advertising to content marketing strategy.

Previous titles from Heather include *Essential Online Advertising: Spend Wisely, Get Results* (2014) and *Email Marketing Success: Build Trust, Win Customers* (2015), both available from oodlebooks.com.

Introduction

When you make the strategic decision to start a blog that will help to generate interest and leads for your business, you are joining literally tens of millions of people around the world who have done exactly the same thing.

So you are not alone in your ambitions and the journey you're about to go on is one that has been completed successfully many times before.

This is great news because it means that there are almost unlimited resources out there for you to tap into to help you achieve your goals for a new business blog. Whether it is technical information, problem-solving, strategy or creativity you need help with, the Internet has an abundance of blogging "how to" riches you can exploit, direct from people who really have been there and done it.

But you don't need to worry about researching at the minute, because the basics you need to make a great start are contained in this guide. All you do need right now is the desire to create a blogging strategy and then set things up so that you can confidently get started....plus the determination to stick at it.

I guarantee that once you have got your new blog up and running, a couple of months down the line you will wonder what all the fuss was about. Yes it can be intimidating when you first start, but your learning curve is going to be far less steep by using this guide.

In this guide you are going to learn:

- What the benefits of blogging are
- How to create a blogging strategy
- How to tap into and develop your brand through blogging
- The exact technical steps you should follow to create a scalable blog
- The do's and don'ts of creating content people will want to read and share
- Building your audience
- How to build and exploit an email list

Before we crack on I just want to make the point that this blog creation guide will start out with the basics and then get progressively more involved. This is necessary in order to give you the best chance of success.

Because of this, it is vital that you don't try and cut corners or do things too quickly. When bolted together, everything in this guide will create a comprehensive "big picture" that will work for anyone. The truth is that shortcuts don't pay off when creating online infrastructure for the long-term.

Part One: Developing a Blogging Strategy

Writing a blog that resonates with people interested in your product or service has many benefits, as long as you go about developing your blog content and structure intelligently.

Creating a unique angle in your industry can be a fantastic way to build a network of people around you, both those looking for your product or service and also other people who have the same or complimentary businesses.

Blogging is also about taking control. You are building online infrastructure for the long-term to benefit your business for the long-term. It is a platform for you to market from, building up a body of high quality content that will bring you visitors through the following channels:

1. People who have searched on a topic and landed on your blog article from a search engine.
2. People who have become fans of what you write and who read everything you publish.
3. People who have found you through social media.

4. People who have been referred to your blog by others who are fans of your information.

Not only does blogging allow you to take control by building a platform, but it also helps to "future proof" you against search engine changes.

Google is famous for moving the goalposts frequently. Entire businesses have been destroyed overnight through changes made by Google to their search algorithm. One day your site is ranking well, the next it's disappeared. Fewer visitors means fewer leads, which means fewer sales.

By taking a unique angle within your industry you can create an audience that is not driven to you solely through search engines. By offering valuable information on your blog you can help to offset any future issues around your organic search engine traffic by pulling in potential customers to your blog from a variety of sources, especially through social media and building an email list.

Is It Worth Starting Another Blog In My Industry?

One of the first objections you will need to overcome in your own mind is the perfectly reasonable assumption that every possible topic has been done to death.

The truth is that although there are millions of blogs out there, most of them are of a low standard in terms of the value they provide.

People are always desperate to find and follow a blog that offers high quality information around a topic, product or service they are interested in.

If you can tap into an angle consistently, with a unique and appealing voice, then it doesn't matter how saturated an industry is, there will always be room for you. In starting a blog, you are starting a long-term information marketing campaign.

Let Me Tell You Exactly What a Blog Is... And Is Not!

The great thing about blogging is that the entry point can be very low cost and incredibly well supported, both in terms of software and support networks.

But in order to tap into this successfully, you need to understand exactly what a blog is, technically and as an information tool.

In technical terms, a blog is just a website. We will cover specific software you can use later on, but generally you can blog using any platform. So don't worry about how you're going to find and use specific blogging software. The truth is that any software that can build a website can be used as a blog.

In terms of providing information, blog content is not the same as information you would put on your main website. Blogging should be personal and valuable information sharing, not just an extension of the promotional language you use on your website.

This is a key point that needs to be fully appreciated if you are to be successful in blogging about your business. If you see your blog purely as a conversion tool then you will fail. If you see your blog as a way of connecting personally with potential and existing customers, then you will stand a far greater chance of success.

There are far too many company blogs out there that are just stuffed full of sales and marketing messages, press releases and impersonal filler articles. Go down this road and you are literally wasting your time.

If you can develop a valuable blog, delivered from a personal angle, then you can establish yourself as a resource in that industry. A 'go-to' person; even an expert. By establishing this reputation through blogging, you can convince more people than before that your company is the one they should buy from.

Creating a Detailed Content Marketing Plan for Your New Blog

Blogging is pure content marketing. It is sharing information that will be of genuine use to people and encourage them to share that information to a wider audience effort-free.

In order for you to be successful in this, your blog needs to be written following a clear strategic plan – a content marketing plan.

The first step is to understand clearly who you want to appeal to and what you want them to do after they have finished consuming your content. It's a great idea to ask yourself some general questions at this point:

- What do I want people to think when they visit my blog?
- How do I want people to interact with it?
- What demographics am I targeting?
- What action do I want them to take after reading an article?
- How can I position myself differently to competing blogs?

In short – you need to know who your customers and potential customers are.

You also need to decide the broad topics you are going to cover. People follow blogs that offer information they are interested in. If you simply create a general blog that rambles on about various, loosely related topics then you have to ask why would anybody be interested? Would you be?

Let's say that you sell blue widgets.

Have a look at what other people in the industry are doing with their blogs about the delights of blue widgets and look for an angle nobody is covering correctly. You are looking for a genuine gap, your point of difference that can draw readers to your blog like moths to a flame.

Even if there is no genuine gap, you can look for angles that are not covered very well. No matter how many people are blogging, there will always be a place for your blog's content if you look hard enough. Look at what is on offer and ask yourself what information potential customers would benefit from.

Gather as much information as you can through asking questions and researching. You can then start to construct a detailed content marketing plan for your blog.

Your plan can map out the topics you will cover, from what angle and how they will link together. For example, you could create a series of articles around a single question people routinely ask you.

Once you have written these articles and have published them on your new blog, one great strategy to reuse content is to bundle them together into a single free PDF download. This can help you to build a mailing list more rapidly.

Throughout your planning, you should be looking at creating a content plan that seeks to answer genuine questions that people always ask within your business niche. This will create highly targeted content that will answer those questions for the long-term. This is called "Evergreen" content and planning to create as much of it as possible will be of huge benefit.

Just to give you a quick example of what we mean by evergreen content, it would be great to create an article around the key benefits of blue widgets. It wouldn't be so great to write about the benefits of blue widgets in the current economic climate of 2015 as this would soon be out-of-date.

Decide Exactly What Action You Want People to Take

At the end of the content planning process you should have a really solid plan for what you are going to publish and why it will help people when you do publish it.

But before you start writing any content it is vital that you have a general conversion goal nailed down.

Through your content marketing plan you will know what topics you will cover and how they will help people. Now it's important that you are fully clear on the outcome you desire for the person reading it, so that you can build it into your writing.

Just being informed is not enough. They need to be inspired to take a specific action after reading. It could be to join your mailing list, it could be to follow you on social media, it could be to comment on the post, it could be to click through to your main website.

An important point here is that the action they take is never to buy. You are building relationships through blogging that can lead to a sale. Blogging is about getting people to know you, like you and trust you, not to try and push them into buying immediately. That will leave them cold and make them feel exploited.

It is better to see your blog as part of the top of your sales funnel. It is an informal lead generation tool that can ease people into the top compartment of the funnel.

To make it crystal clear, blogging is not about selling, it's about building relationships. If you go into this thinking that your blog is a sales tool then you will fail. A blog is an informal information resource that builds trust in you as an authority and encourages people to further consider the products or services you offer.

Building a Blogging Brand

Your company probably already has its own brand. The logo, certain colours, service promises, and maybe even certain language you use.

Blogging should be personal. Ideally, it should be written by you as an individual. This goes back to building relationships. If it's a faceless corporate blog then it will feel cold and people will not form an emotional attachment.

So consider how you're going to market yourself within the blogging brand you are creating. Use an appealing photo, think about sharing personal information, perhaps through weaving relevant personal anecdotes into your writing.

Think about the style of writing you will employ. How will your writing style draw people in and keep them interested? Use certain phrases, refer back to previous key stories or strategies, anything that keeps people emotionally linked to you and draws them closer to buying from you.

The best blogs are those that people get emotionally attached to. If you can tap into a unique industry angle to deliver high quality information while personally appealing to people then you stand a great chance of building a long-term lead generation tool for your business.

Part Two: Technical Implementation

Before we talk through the technical implementation of your new blog, we need to first discuss how the type of blog you create can dictate your future plans.

Many people overlook the importance of the decision they have to make around the software platform they use to blog from.

The truth is that one of the biggest decisions you have to make at the start of this process is to decide on the software you're going to use. Get it right and you can develop in any way you please, get it wrong and you will soon feel trapped.

The Choice: Hosted or Self-Hosted Blog Software?

First, it's important we clarify something which confuses a lot of people who are thinking about setting up a blog for the first time.

A blog is a website. It really is that simple.

Although platforms that call themselves blog software have built-in features to make publishing content easy, there is essentially no difference between a website and a blog.

The truth is that you can use specialist blogging software to create a company website, just as you can use it to create a dedicated blog.

At the heart of this confusion lays the well-known blogging software WordPress.

Although WordPress was developed originally as blogging software, it now has so many built in features, themes and frameworks, plus plugins to increase functionality, that it is now capable of developing any type of website, from a simple blog through to a massive e-commerce website.

This takes us to the choice you have to make: do you start a hosted, or self-hosted blog?

A hosted blog is one you don't install on your own web space. You don't need to download software, you don't need to get your hands dirty in code.

A hosted blog is one provided for you on websites such as blogger.com and WordPress.com. You simply sign up for an account and are given instant access to an admin area that allows you basic features to produce a website/blog.

A self-hosted blog is one where you own web space and install software on it that you have to manage yourself. This involves paying for a web hosting package through a hosting provider. Some of the bigger ones you might want to consider are Cloudnext, Heart Internet, 123-Reg.

The trap many people fall into is to run away from having to deal with the technical side of things. It's far easier to create an account on a hosted platform and start blogging quickly, than it is start messing around installing software.

The problem is that the lack of features and power make hosted blogs a terrible option for the long-term. You don't know what the future holds for your new blog so boxing yourself into a platform that simply cannot cope with expansion, or will cost money to expand, is a poor strategy that many regret.

So my recommendation is always to take a deep breath and embrace the process of setting up your own blog on your own web space, in order to ensure your long-term future.

Let's Talk About WordPress

WordPress is the most powerful blogging software in the world and the most widely used. Some people claim that download statistics show that WordPress powers more than a quarter of the websites currently online.

Whether that is true or not, it does point to the dominance of this platform.

The reason it is so dominant is down to several key reasons:

- It is free to download and use
- There are thousands of free functionality extensions known as plugins available
- There are thousands of free themes to tailor the way your website looks in a few clicks
- Nearly every webhosting company in the world supports it fully
- There is a massive online community that can help you free of charge

- The way it is structured means that most people can tweak code to get what they want
- There are so many WordPress developers out there that hiring costs are driven down

Just to clear up another area of confusion, I want to make it clear that there are two versions of WordPress available:

1. There is a hosted version on WordPress.com. This is where you create an account and have access to a basic version of the WordPress software. The problem is that upgrades, such as using your own domain name and turning on extra plugins all cost money.

2. There is a downloadable software version of WordPress available from WordPress.org. This is the software you can install on your web server and manage yourself (AKA 'self-hosted').

So to take control of your blogging and have access to all of the features that WordPress can offer you will need to embrace the self-hosted version. This means getting your own web space and installing the software.

But don't worry, it's not as difficult as it sounds to set up your own self hosted WordPress blog and I'm going to talk you through it step-by-step right now.

How to Install a Self-Hosted WordPress Blog

1. Get some web space.
You may already have web space if you have a company website. If you do then it will be best to install your new blog in a subdirectory, for example:

yoursite.com/blog/

Or you might install it as a subdirectory:

blog.yoursite.com

If you don't have web space available then there are plenty of low-cost webhosts out there, such as Cloudnext, Heart Internet and Dreamhost who we have already mentioned, where monthly hosting costs less than $10 (even less if you search online for coupon codes, I recently picked up a year of shared hosting on Dreamhost for $22, which is around £14)

2. Add a domain name.

If you already have a domain name attached to your main company website then you can skip this step as the blog will be installed in a subdirectory, or subdomain of your main site.

If you don't have a website then you will need to register a domain name with a registrar such as Godaddy, 123-Reg or Name. You will then need to make sure this domain name is entered when you sign up for your new web space account.

If you need to get a domain name to set-up a blog on a webhosting account, then the webhost will have a support area and people you can contact to help you.

3. Install the core WordPress software.

There are two ways that you can install the WordPress software. The first way is the more complicated. You visit WordPress.org, download a copy and then use another piece of software (an FTP program) to upload it to your main site. Then you create a database and link the two together.

I'm hoping you don't have to go down that road, but if you do then there are plenty of tutorials on the Internet to help with this manual installation process, including on the main WordPress.org site, and it really is not as tough to do as it sounds.

The easier option is to look inside your hosting accounts control panel. Most large webhosting companies offer what are known as "one click installs" on the more popular software, including WordPress. You should literally be able to click a button and have WordPress installed on your server.

Once installed you will be sent an email and be able to click on a link to enter some admin login details so you can get started.

Using Plugins to Extend the Power of Your Blog

After you've installed WordPress there will be some plugins you need to install to ensure your new blog has all the features it needs.

A plugin is basically extended functionality for your new blog. There are literally thousands of them available from the main WordPress.org site. Whatever you want to do there is usually a free plugin that can achieve it.

Please don't get carried away installing dozens of plugins that you don't really need. The truth is that for a basic blog set up you only need a handful of key plugins:

1. A contact form plugin. This will allow you to create forms and embed them into pages on your new site, for example a form for people to contact you through. The two most popular are Contact Form 7 and SI Contact Form.

2. A SEO plugin. The most popular WordPress SEO plugin is from a developer known as Yoast. It used to be called the Yoast SEO plugin, but is now simply known as WordPress SEO. When installed, this will allow you to have granular control over options such as whether pages are visited and indexed by search engines, how titles are presented to Google and the creation of sitemaps. To make things even easier for a novice, the plugin also has a traffic light system to help you see how changes you are making effect the optimisation of your content.

3. A related posts plugin. This will display related content at the bottom of each of your articles. It is a great way of getting people who have visited your blog to stay on it and read more of your content. What related posts are displayed is decided by the plugin, meaning you don't have to intervene at all to display fresh content to your visitors.

4. A spam filter plugin. I'm just going to say activate and use Akismet here. This is a plugin that comes with WordPress as standard. It does a great job at filtering out spam comments and preventing admin logins.

5. A social sharing plugin. There are dozens of options out there, such as Mashshare or Social Media Feather, which add social sharing options into your articles, allowing people to share them on social networks such as Facebook and Twitter.

In addition to the above I would also suggest you install a security plugin. The one I would recommend is Wordfence. It is free to use and will protect you against attackers trying to log into your admin area and it runs security scans to make sure the integrity of your blog is not compromised – emailing you if it finds file changes for example.

On top of that, Wordfence has a built in caching engine. Caching is a process where the plugin makes a copy of each page to deliver, rather than relying on your web server building the page every time it is requested by the visitor. This massively speeds up delivery of content pages to visitors and takes stress off your server.

The Wordfence engine is literally a one click install and can boost the speed of your site loading massively.

One last word on plugins, you might want to install a plug-in called Jetpack. This is a suite of plugins brought together under one umbrella plugin. It is developed and maintained by WordPress themselves, so it is trustworthy and always up-to-date with the latest version of the core WordPress software.

Jetpack contains around 30 different individual plugins you can activate from one admin screen, including contact forms, social sharing options, additional login security, image caching and even the ability to record and deliver stats on visitors within your WordPress admin panel.

So it's a powerful plugin and worth looking at as it addresses several of your key needs in one package.

Whatever plugins you decide to use, these can be installed quickly and easily through your WordPress admin panel.

You simply visit the *Plugins* link in your admin panel, click on *Add New*, and search by plugin name and click *Install*. The plugin will then be downloaded and activated in your admin panel for you to configure.

A Quick Tour of the Main WordPress Features and Options You Need to know.

I'm not going to bore you by going through every single option contained in the WordPress admin panel. However there are a small number of things that you really do need to do before you start blogging.

The first is to change your permalink structure. Permalinks are basically the way your blog URLs are structured. We want them to be search engine friendly, so we need to change them from the default setting which uses numbers, rather than descriptive words.

The default looks like this:

http://yourblog.com/p?=123

The structure we want is:

http://yourblog.com/name-of-your-content-title

In the WordPress admin panel, click on **Settings** and then click on **Permalinks**. On that page select the **Post name** option and save.

Doing this will make your content URLs more relevant to people as they can see what the content is about. It also makes the link more search engine friendly.

The second thing you need to do is to set up your commenting policy. This is in the **Settings > Discussion** screen. There you can set a global commenting policy, from not allowing comments at all, through to sending all comments into moderation for you to authorise or delete.

From that screen you can also allow or disallow pingbacks (notifications). This is a feature that is widely abused, so I recommend you just switch it off.

Making Your WordPress Blog Look Great

When you visit a WordPress blog it will have a certain layout and use certain colours. The way it looks is down to the theme that the blog uses for its layout, colours and navigational structure.

There are literally tens of thousands of WordPress themes available on the Internet. Many of them are completely free. You can find an army of free themes in the WordPress theme repository (https://WordPress.org/themes/).

As well as free themes there are thousands of premium ones. These can range in price from a few dollars up to more than one hundred. You are paying for more polished designs, more features built into the theme and developer support post-purchase.

To avoid being overwhelmed by the choice, you need to nail down how you want your new blog to look in terms of layout and colours. There are lots of extra features in some themes, such as image sliders and other fancy stuff, so you need to decide how important such things are to you.

Sketch out how you imagine the blog looking on a piece of paper. The number of columns, specific features and where they will appear.

You can then usually find something very close to what you are looking for, and often completely free.

Another option is to use a theme framework such as Genesis or Thesis. A framework for WordPress is a base of code which sits underneath the theme. It runs all the essentials of the blog and links to what is known as a "child theme" which controls the way it looks.

The benefit of a framework is that you can update it when a new version becomes available, without overwriting the original theme files.

When you use a normal WordPress theme any changes you make to the core files will be overwritten when you update the theme to a new version – there is no separation between how a site looks and how it acts. Themes and plugins are often updated by their authors to make sure they work with the latest version of the WordPress software, so it is a vital consideration.

So using a framework linked to a child theme can save a lot of headache in the long run.

But don't worry if that all sounds too advanced, to get started you can simply pick a theme that looks good, install it and get blogging in a matter of minutes.

Another thing to bear in mind is that your theme needs to work in all sizes of screen. With more people viewing sites through tablets and mobile phones, I recommend you only look for themes which are labelled as 'responsive'. This means they are fluid and adjust automatically depending on the size of window they are viewed in.

You install themes in exactly the same way as you install plugins. From within your WordPress admin panel (under *Appearance > Themes* and *Add New*) search for the name of the theme and click install, then click to activate it. Job done.

Once installed every theme has certain options you can edit from inside the WordPress admin area (usually within the Appearance menu, but occasionally a theme will create its own menu link when installed). You can do things like add a custom header image, change navigation menus and alter the colours of your blog.

Of course, if you pick a theme which looks just right for you then you can get away with not changing anything at all.

A great tip is to remember that when you change options in a theme or plugin, those changes are saved in the WordPress database. You can deactivate a plugin or theme and when you reactivate it, the settings will be remembered. So you can experiment with different themes and plugins without losing the settings every time.

Working With Wonderful WordPress Widgets.

Wow, what a title. Say it out loud a few times.

Thankfully, once you get past the name, widgets are an incredibly easy way to have complete control over how your new blog will look and interact with visitors.

Widgets generally control what appear in the side columns and footer of your blog, although some modern themes have widget areas all over the place.

When you look at a WordPress theme, there are usually two columns. The first column is the main content column where you will read the blog content that has been published. To the right or left you will see a thinner column, called a sidebar.

Everything displayed in the sidebars is controlled by widgets.

Widgets allow you to have granular control over how your sidebars operate. Simply by dragging and dropping a widget to your sidebar in your admin panel (Admin > Appearance > Widgets) you can add all sorts of different features to your blog.

The best way to learn about widgets is simply to get in there and play around them. Just like plugins and themes there are also additional widgets available for download. Again you can search for these using Google or visit WordPress.org and search the plugins repository.

Widgets are a great way of adding social functions to your blog, such as the Facebook like boxes, with the faces of people who have liked your site that you see everywhere online nowadays. You can construct various Facebook interactivity options at their developer site (https://developers.facebook.com/products/) and then simply paste the resulting code snippet into a WordPress sidebar widget and save it.

Part Three: Creating Content That Makes People Care and Share

At this point you should have your WordPress blog set-up on your own web space, giving you full control of your blogging future.

On top of that, you should also now have a strategy around what you are going to blog about, your angle, who will benefit from the information you share and what action you want those people to take after reading.

Now it's time to start writing your content.

Your goal is to create content that people will want to read. It needs to be so good that they will come back to read more. They also need to be so impressed by what you're writing that they feel compelled to share it with other like-minded people via social media.

This is no small challenge.

But don't worry, you won't develop your blogging style overnight. It will take months of writing, over dozens of blog entries for you to explore and finalise your style.

One point to make is that you don't have to constantly publish blog content. You will read that Google loves lots of fresh and detailed content. This has led many people into the trap of feeling they have to blog almost daily in order to attract the attention of the search engines.

The truth is that Google is looking for high quality content that explores a topic in-depth in a natural fashion and offers value to the reader. It's better to blog once a week and produce a couple of thousand words of really great content than to churn out 1000 words a day of low quality content.

Don't write for Google, create great content for the people who will read your blog.

How to Quickly Plan a Blog Post

From the plan you created at the start of this process you will have a broad idea around the topics you want to address in your blog articles.

So pick a topic and brainstorm individual subjects you can write about. Pick one of those subjects and consider your angle by asking yourself the following questions:

- What will you be offering the reader?
- Why will they want to read your blog post?
- Are you going to offer detailed advice, or a specific solution to a problem?
- Will the position you take be controversial?
- What is the reaction you are expecting?
- What do you want them to do next (action taken)?

Once you have a clear idea of why this piece will be written then you need to get the structure mapped out on paper.

Start by brainstorming titles. Any half decent copywriter will tell you that the headline is the most important thing to consider. Many copywriters spend more time coming up with a great title than they do on writing the rest of the content.

The objective of your title is to get people to read the first paragraph, so it needs to be interesting and compelling. Look at titles of blogs in your industry covering the same topic and see how you can improve on the headlines they use.

There is obviously a lot more to writing your blog post then I can outline in this guide. To get some fantastic help on writing great web content then the resource I would suggest you look at is copyblogger.com.

Once you have a title, come up with the points you want to make in the article. Usually you will want to make 2-3 main points in the article, no more. I would also suggest you aim for around 1000 words, as this is a good length for conveying detailed information while keeping it easy to read in a few minutes – especially on the move using a small browser screen.

So now you have a title and detail of the main points you want to make it's time to consider your "hook".

You are literally going to plan how you will hook people into reading your piece all the way through. Once they have read your great headline then you need to hit them with a fantastic opening paragraph, with the goal of getting them to continue to read the article.

This means that your opening paragraph has to get them involved. It needs to ask a question they are desperate to find out the answer to, or it needs to be the start of the story that they want to continue reading.

Stories are great for conveying ideas and getting people to buy into reading all the way through to a conclusion that they hope will also help them.

People also like product reviews, so if you can create a story around how your product or service helped someone to succeed, through telling a story about their journey, then that is the sort of structure that creates blogging gold.

In summary, you should aim for each blog post to:

- Attract the reader to read the opening paragraph through a great headline
- Encourage them to continue reading by hooking them in through your first paragraph
- Use storytelling to show a journey from failure to success wherever possible
- Contain enough detail for people to take the next step
- Contain a compelling call to action by knowing exactly what action you want them to take

Developing Your Own Blogging Style

In order to stand out from the crowd you need to take a unique angle and write in a way that people associate with and enjoy.

In short, you need to use a writing style and share information in a way that creates a tribe. People are tribal and by using a style that attracts the right people, you can create loyalty from your growing tribe.

Blogging is an informal style of writing. Sometimes blogging is not even grammatically correct, or structured as it should be. You should think of blogging more as somebody talking to you informally.

That's why a lot of good bloggers recommend using voice recognition software to get that conversational style into the writing.

If you have a very formal and traditional style of writing then using voice recognition software can produce a more relaxed style of article that you can then edit and publish.

Developing your own blogging style will also be about seeking out and reacting to feedback. You will need to look for reaction on social media, get the input of family, friends, colleagues and customers.

It is also vital to look at your statistics. By hooking your blog up to a Google Analytics account you will be able to see which posts are visited most and which posts people spend the most time reading.

When linked up to social media activity, through seeing which of your blog posts is shared the most, you can start to learn which of your articles is hitting the spot. You can then analyse the style used and the content you delivered in order to replicate it for future posts.

Learn To Walk Away Before Hitting Publish

Once you have a great draft article, walk away from it for a least a few days. Forget about it, so that when you come back to it you are almost reading it through fresh eyes.

I guarantee that no matter how good you thought it was, you will end up chopping it around again.

One thing you have to acknowledge and accept from the start is that no content will ever be perfect.

Accepting that your blogging will not be perfect is actually the easiest way to liberate your writing and produce better content in the long term. When your mind is free of pressure you will find that you construct and create far more easily and to a higher standard.

Great blogging is not about being perfect, it is about conveying a compelling point of view that other people want to read and share.

By walking away you give yourself time to refresh and move on, allowing you to come back to your content with a new perspective.

I would suggest you set a goal to write a blog post once per week. Write your first post and then walk away from it for a week. Finalise it and publish it, then write your next piece and repeat the process.

What If I Really Cannot Write Blog Content To Save My Life?

The first thing I would say is to give it a go. Read sites like copyblogger.com, look at the style of sites in your niche that you want to compete against and just go for it.

Once you have written a piece pass it on to people for feedback. The main thing to remember is that you will not be brilliant straight away and as with any skill it will take time to learn and master.

Especially at the start, you will not have much of a readership, so use the first few months as a learning curve for yourself and work hard to develop your own style and analyse your experiences.

If you simply can't do it, or you cannot find the time to do it, then you will have to look at outsourcing the work to a reliable writer.

There are several sites out there which will allow you to hire good quality content writers, including those who are experienced bloggers. Elance.com, oDesk.com and Freelancer.com are three of the biggest and the places where some of the best affordable writers congregate.

In terms of cost, the golden rule is to not hunt out your ghost-writer purely on the price they charge.

Let's be clear here, five dollar content is going to be dull at best, and stolen or "spun" (where base content has words substituted to create partially fresh content), at worst. Quality blogs regularly pay rates of around $30-$50 (£20-£40) per 500 words for good content.

Now I'm not saying you need to go that high in price, especially in the beginning, but if you are thinking that $10 (around £6) per 500 words is a lot of money then your blog is not going to contain great content. As with anything else in life, you get what you pay for.

Writing is an investment – whether you create it yourself or pay someone else to do it, you want your blog content to rank and bring customers for years to come.

Once you have chosen a writer, give them a trial. Contract them to publish one post a week for a month in order for you to both bed-in and get comfortable. At the end of that time review progress and if things are going well, ask them to write a post a week on an ongoing basis.

By doing this, you will be able to get good quality content from somebody who is starting to understand your business and what you are trying to achieve through your blog. If you can't write the blog content yourself, then creating a strategy with somebody you trust is a great substitute.

Build Your Audience.

As a novice blogger it's important you focus on the quality of your content and take your time creating it. Great content will bring visitors. As long as it is on topic, highly relevant and infectiously shareable, your traffic will grow.

Now that does not mean you should expect 1000 visitors a day. Just by creating great content you might get 10 to 100 people a day in a few months from search engine visitors.

But don't get disheartened. Over time this will grow. As your readership grows and you develop your blogs content style, it will be shared in wider and wider circles, but only if you offer valuable insight and information as well.

There are of course extra things you can do to build your audience. The main way you can build it quickly is through social media. Twitter and Facebook are great ways to increase the readership of your blog.

Don't be a marketer, don't spam and don't act like a brand. Be yourself. Start conversations, join conversations and add value to the social circles you are moving in. By doing this people will become curious about you and visit the blog.

One great piece of advice is to look for influencers in the niche your blog covers. There is always a small group of people at the centre of a niche who are followed by many others. Getting your foot in the door with these people can rapidly increase the rate at which your content is shared.

Build A List. Now.

If you are aiming to make money from your new WordPress blog then it is advisable that you also start building an email list from the start.

Even if you aren't selling anything now, or your blog is not about profit, harvesting the email addresses of interested people is always beneficial somewhere down the line.

Bottom line is – build a list. No matter what you think now – build a list.

There are lots of options out there for building mailing lists; some are free, some you have to pay for. All of them do basically the same thing.

One thing you need to be aware of before you make the decision on which option to use, is what future development you will do on your blog.

If you only intend to collect email addresses to communicate with or market to, then you can use a mailing list plugin linked to a provider such as Mailchimp or Aweber.

Mailchimp offers a free account for up to 2000 subscribers, and can be linked to a WordPress plugin. Just search for Mailchimp in your WordPress admin area's add new plugin page.

Aweber is a paid option. It also uses a plugin to display the subscription form and process subscriptions on your blog.

If you intend to develop your blog into something more in the future, then you might want to consider starting to gather your mailing list in the form of membership accounts. The process is exactly the same but you will need more powerful software (such as eMember or Digital Access Pass) which store the information in your own database rather than with a third party.

Although more expensive, the bonus is that at any stage you can turn your blog into a powerful membership site. People who subscribed to your mailing list will have instant access, meaning they don't have to sign up again – giving you instant members.

If you don't want a members site, these plugins can also do more powerful things than simple subscription options. Crucially they can act as autoresponders, delivering a timed sequence of emails after the initial sign-up. This is great for drip-feeding people with emails that offer a piece of compelling advice and encouraging them to click through to find out more.

Whichever option you choose, it is usual practice to provide something for free in return for somebody completing the subscription form. This could take the form of access to download an ebook or generate a sequence of automated information emails.

We talked earlier about creating a downloadable product from your existing blog content – a key reason why it's important that each piece is created as part of a content strategy and not written in isolation.

You will also need to consider what to feed the subscriber once they have signed up. It could simply be notifications of new post on your blog, it could be a multi-part course, or exclusive offers. All this can be done if you use an autoresponder.

Dealing with Problems

There will be times during the set-up and early days of your new blogging career where you hit problems.

Whatever happens - don't panic! Remember that whatever you are experiencing has been seen and solved a thousand times before.

The most obvious place to get help for anything related to the technical side of your blog is to open a support ticket with your web hosting provider. Most providers also have community forums where you can discuss things and get best practice.

For WordPress specific help the most obvious place is the WordPress.org forums. You can ask as many questions you like on there. There are thousands of experienced WordPress users on there who can help you with your problem.

More generally, a search on Google for the problem you are facing will usually bring up several highly relevant results to help you. There are also hundreds of WordPress help sites on the net which have lots of valuable information on them, as well as YouTube videos if you want visual help and walk-throughs.

Whatever happens, don't panic. Don't give up. Take your time and learn as you go.

Just Go For It!

With this guide and some time and effort you can own a blog that hundreds, if not thousands of people will flock to read every day.

You will encounter problems and barriers, but lots of people have been through the same thing and by sticking at it are the owners of powerful blogs.

Most bloggers who give up do so within the first three months.

A lot of others have nothing to show for their initial work, other than an empty blog and a load of passwords, plus money being debited from their account each month.

To succeed you will need four things:

1. Control. That means being self-hosted.
2. Direction. Get a unique voice and angle.
3. Persistence. You will have rough patches, so fight through them.
4. Balance. Use your time wisely between producing good content, development planning and marketing.

It is not as tough as you think it will be to set-up and run a WordPress blog. You can do it and the results can create a source of publicity and income for your business for the long term.

Good Luck!

Heather

Find out more about digital marketing for small business on my blog: http://skitti.sh/blog

Connect with me on Twitter @_skittish

Find more resources online:
http://skittish.academy